TO AND FROM

AHSAHTA PRESS

The New Series

NUMBER 22

TO AND FROM

G. E. PATTERSON

AHSAHTA PRESS

BOISE STATE UNIVERSITY · BOISE · IDAHO · 2008

Ahsahta Press, Boise State University
Boise, Idaho 83725
http://ahsahtapress.boisestate.edu

Copyright © 2008 by G. E. Patterson
Printed in the United States of America
Cover design by Quemadura
Cover art: Jess, American (1923-2004). *Figure 2 – A Field of Pumpkins Grown For Seed: Translation #11*, 1965. Oil on canvas (mounted on wood), 29½ × 36 inches (74.9 × 91.4 cm). The Nelson-Atkins Museum of Art, Kansas City, Missouri. Purchase: acquired through the generosity of the William T. Kemper Foundation – Commerce Bank, Trustee, 2006.26. Photograph by Jamison Miller. ©2008 the Jess Collins Trust. Used by permission.
Author photo ©2007 by JoAnn Verburg
Book design and typography by Janet Holmes
First printing March 2008
ISBN-13: 978-0-916272-99-9

Library of Congress Cataloging-in-Publication Data

Patterson, G. E.
To and from / G. E. Patterson.
p. cm. -- (The new series ; no. 22)
ISBN 978-0-916272-99-9 (pbk. : alk. paper)
I. Title.

PS3566.A819T62 2008
811'.54—dc22
                            2007018596

ACKNOWLEDGMENTS

My thanks to the editors and readers of the following journals where pages from this manuscript have been published: *American Letters and Commentary* ("The Hotel Room," "Curiosity, Tenderness, Kindness, Ecstasy"); *Aphrodite of the Spangled Mind* ("We Said to Someone"); *Fence* ("Early Winter," "L'Histoire: Sad Chair: A History;") *Five Fingers Review* ("Salvator Mundi"); *MiPoesias* ("Continuous: Interruption," "A Temporary Spot," "In Berlin: Secret Agent Man"); *nocturnes (re) view of the arts* ("Yes between that Thank You," "The Yellow Wood," "Fantasie C-dur"); *Open City* ("Drift//Land"); *Provincetown Arts* ("A Certain Mood Invented by Candlelight"); *St. Mark's Poetry Project Poets and Poems* ("Who Goes There," "Biceps of Longing," "As If That Alone," "Hesitation Step," "It Has a Back"); *Seneca Review* ("How Could One Contemplate Paradise without . . .," "Tender Burglar Stranger"); *Swerve* (Starlit, Pictures of Square Flat Lawns and Oblong Trees, "Once Again, That Famous Syndrome," "It May Happen," "Nocturne," "Imaginations of the Ch'an Experience"); *Waterstone Review* ("Glib Pirouette Out of Messiness"); *WinteRed* ("from Mulberry Street"); *Xcp: Cross Cultural Poetics* ("Radiant Folly," "Late and Early Sensation," "Rain," "The Maiden Several Hours Later," "Salvation Remedy," "Light . . .Who Sees It," "Here, It's Coming").

for W. S. DiPiero (again)

"Perhaps . . . ."

— Virginia Woolf

". . . today . . . ."

— Elizabeth Alexander

Contents

New York Suite

    Radiant Folly   5

    Rain   6

    A Certain Mood Invented by Candlelight   7

    Starlit   8

    Salvation Remedy   9

    Here, It's Coming   10

    Pictures of Square, Flat Lawns and Oblong Trees   11

    Early Winter   12

    Once Again, That Famous Syndrome   13

    Immortal Life   14

    "How Could One Contemplate Paradise Without . . . ."   15

    It May Happen   16

    Nocturne   17

    Imaginations of the Ch'an Experience   18

    A Train Comes   19

    House, Ghost, Image, Color   20

Give or Take

    Tender Burglar Stranger   23

    Baby Tears   24

    Which Is the Dream   25

    "Glib Pirouette out of Messiness"   26

    Late and Early Sensation   27

    Faith—The Thing with Faith   28

    (Hope) and Parade   29

    Before or after but Not in between   30

    The Maiden Several Hours Later   31

    Light . . . Who Sees It   32

    The Hotel Room   33

A Big Long Gabled Corridor   34
Yes between That Thank You   35
Revolving toward What Is Not a Thing   36
Flowers on Your Path   37
"Curiosity, Tenderness, Kindness, Ecstasy"   38

Mulberry Street

L'Histoire: Sad Chair: A History   41
Who Goes There?   42
The Yellow Wood   43
Biceps of Longing   44
As If That Alone   45
Hesitation Step: 46
It Has a Back   47
Salvator Mundi   48
Butter Sultana Biscuits   49
Fantasie C–dur   50
That Rose before Me   51
What Remains Comfort   52
Those Things which Were Not Ambiguities   53
Natural and Imaginary Objects   54
Apparatus for Distillation   55
The Rescue Party   56

Cape Cod

Pail of Water   59
Undisturbing Distance   60
Another Happy Story   61
Perhaps No Longer Than That All   62
Wherever We Are Going Are We Almost   63
John Button Has a Pretty Name   64
People, the Woods   65

Two People in the Woods   66

For One Instance   67

Hotel-Title: Poem   68

Continuous: Interruption   69

A Temporary Spot   70

In Berlin: Secret Agent Man   71

We Said to Someone   72

Morning Coat   73

Drift/Land   74

About the Author   75

"... opened to sunlight ...."

—Honor Moore

"... another life."

—Gerard de Nerval

"... you?"

"... and touch ...."

—Anne Porter

Perhaps This World and Candy

"... my friend."

—Stephen Spender

Here is the time you might have felt returning
When it was promised it seemed so unreal
You'd find the same things either more or less
On the far coast where waves are known to land
Nothing's crying out because it is not
Like everything else you see in the world
Stuck on the possibility of being
So close to the thing we have longed for softly
In each season you saw that even though
There was no arm leading toward the sea
All the signs the breeze gave were for this turning
Along the way one had often imagined
More differences than were would await us
We might not know ourselves or where we were

New York Suite

The early wishes

"What happens is not . . . ."
　　　　　—Brenda Hillman

". . .find. . . ."
　　　　　—T. S. Eliot

Radiant Folly

". . . cling. . . ."
　　　　　—Ted Joans

The human stacks open to limitation
Invisibility tree swan perhaps
This room seen with a bird's anatomy
You may remember as someone else speaks

Sometimes many things are possible
The hunger for one is common and varied
An effect I notice when someone's near
Where you might go when bad news put on blush

Desires like the horses persist and run
A sense of what becomes pleasant in time
Glad for the weather to be led through this
Maybe the stranger makes the sounds himself
And he hopes when the song begins again
Pulling your wet mouth away from elsewhere

"... now there was. ..."
—Marjorie Kinnan Rawlins

Rain

"Each sentence replaces an hallucination."
—Lyn Hejinian

"... with feelings too. ..."
—T. S. Eliot

Will it rain this afternoon if I don't
Or lines descend in splendor from above
May matter be transformed by belief here
Meaning greened stones meaning it picked the pockets

Undercut by sounds shirtwaist a night blue
Children cast roly poly in lost sand
The dangers of thirst sound like the fresh water
See a little figure wobble their legs are brass

There may not be a good way to love time
It may not be possible to love this
Coming to only ourselves collared birds
Coming to the dream with accurate balance
Patrolling the wail at the ocean's border
: *The land do dry our beauty crack the skin*

                                        Am I scared,
                                        he wants to know,
                                        am I scared

My condition is a poor excuse for that

A Certain Mood Invented by Candlelight
"A power . . . you can stop . . ."
                                        —Brenda Hillman

Say the rain started in the night and stopped
Because it is time and it is important
Continuing the wind lessened with help
The pearl seen in the open mouth of love

The answer is a factory of candles
While for what it's worth the street's hum and glow
Who dreamed up garnet or the color jasper
This light the damp air the encircled body

Yes the wind failed despite the noise it made
The wind dropped beneath a gibbous moon
When the sun's out shadows dominate gardens
This is true: See the sky is a soft gray

The wind died without a line on its face
Before it reached you it was hurrying

" . . . this notion that things start . . ."

—Brenda Hillman

Starlit

whatever that means in another language

Oh my people how quickly tears fill bowls
How easily the heart falls into habits
How many times I am myself and you
Fish and fisherman surrounded by water

An odd way of thinking that grows is green
The light would make spills over everything
Out of a sense of duty the dark darkens
It might be kindness in a perfect world

All the new ditties should be learned and sung
Think and hop and smile do it for your mother
Where are you going lonesome cowboy man
Here is a reason no one will believe
Oh my people how quickly tears fill bowls
I love my dog more when he licks my hand

Salvation Remedy

"In time the . . . faint. . . ."

—Robert Duncan

The whole night sky yellow as are the stars—
You are myself and I the upstairs neighbor
When the orange fir boards gave way at once
Long ago enough to let the air steam
Plausible looks and possessions away.
Not to lie, to begin, by being honest,
Being patient with a plot holding dreams
In which nothing happens to burn the water,

The little boat stays moored in the familiar
Depth of the fictional. Middle age then,
Maybe the text of discourse, its importance,
Attaches itself to the other thing.
But then again it was the other thing
Different too from perfect shapes as one saw.

Not the same thing as

"Bessie's feet hurt"
—Gwendolyn Brooks

Here, It's Coming

". . . ." [unwritten words]
—John Milton

It was like that, a taste of what we want
And wanted so to refuse it as easy;
Fear though, the invitation to it, was,
I mean a smaller problem than the whole,
The way it comes. When it isn't daylight
It was hard and dark to distinguish tree
And the pain from night's foolishness or smarts.
Most of what is shared should be embarrassing

An experience, our own, that differs,
In place details the other little ruins
Whatever is meant by *we* should let go
Even as the wheel spoken of in circles
Without asking the wheel what it thinks of
You don't know what it means to spin, do you?

Something shiny

Pictures of Square, Flat Lawns and Oblong Trees
with history

Although it wants to go to bed with us
And we want more than bodies can contain
The reality is not disappointing
The external voice that says *Here* or *No*
We fail so often it's hard to believe
We have our lists of needs and ways of being
Inimitable to us as our children
With nothing to stop it from happening

Oh yes, definitely, the lights go on
At dusk when everyone's out in the city
Unspeakably blah people appear moving
In a raking light casting funny shadows
So baronial ideas become landscape
We forget how it might be in our sleep

("... everything else ....."

—Linda Gregg)

Early Winter

"... have turned back all ....."

—Henri Coulette

To borrow an old thought that still enlivens
Part of the hosts' pleasure lies in arranging
A picnic item or a get-well wish
Images in the heads of everyone
Resembling themselves only slightly lighter
As trees or stars or room or pussy spark
The smell of something sweet from underneath
Woven baskets of fruit in late December

Another time when the fun was delayed
At the aura of beyond a blue sours
The odor of sweet grass (was) someone mowing
From inside the frame a rose in your picture
Bottled baby's breath the Wilmington room
Coming from the car as it moves what stays

"the past slips into you finally"
—Brenda Hillman

"your hunger was beautiful,
her hunger was beautiful ..."
—Brenda Hillman

Once Again, That Famous Syndrome
reserved for itself

Your hunger was beautiful then my hunger
Kept to itself in a manner of speaking
Like a wind blowing down the road this moment
Like this wind and the original thought
Loneliness we might say if we were talking
In that other country where we are not
Less conscious of being ourselves or pleased
To think our thoughts might be taken as music

As anything else—unsatisfied hopeless
Surprised to find ourselves as we intended
After walking down the short roads that end
With water or gardens or summer light
After gassing a car buying the ticket
Here for the few seconds it takes to slacken

How little the mouth takes to fill with worry

"... the looseness is taken away."
—Brenda Hillman

Immortal Life

"... we are unsatisfied ...."
—Forrest Hamer

"... we look ...."
—Forrest Hamer

If it's not quite the same it can be said
In some sense to be changing what we think
Is the world its meaning and so our minds
Try to separate a thing from itself

Good or bad depends on stories you know
Methods and ideals that might have been taken
By the heart leading to what is a shift
In talk, or in certain places, a joke

Chinese rabbit noises echo a coldness
So charged you closed off hearing as a child
The same principles may apply to seeing
The breath of someone else perhaps we know
More or less, still, a body, hard to grasp
How you would feel to find yourself in Denmark

Wait! Wait! Wait!

"... there isn't a residue ...."
—Robert Motherwell

"How Could One Contemplate Paradise Without ...."
—Lyn Hejinian

"... we sit on a slope to admire."
—Lyn Hejinian

Someone must be feeling exactly what
Even though what we suppose may not be
Although perhaps sometimes it does enough
What Susan attributes to molecules

Phenomena often termed quaintly spiritual
The development of which is a thing
Open dangers the thing cannot secure
More or less we are reflections of risk

Associated with our own emotions
The boom and strut and dairy smell of pleasure
As in most memories of childhood lies
With truth a close equivalent of landscape
Whether we care to give up or hold on
A felt backdrop projected past and passing

"Here and there . . . ."
　　　　　—T. S. Eliot

". . . for a particular point of view—"
　　　　　—Lyn Hejinian

It May Happen

　　as though it doesn't matter what is real

". . . something almost . . . with asking."
　　　　　—Brenda Hillman

According to their signs we're in the country
Far off things are being put on the record
Where it may not matter to anyone
If the shadows hide themselves behind rain
The canal opening below the sky
Daytime moving in swirls the painted colors
Or the idea wind sometimes stops and starts
What we might more properly call nostalgia

If we wanted to we could follow later
Without giving up his place in the world
A color postcard folded in our pockets
The light informing us it's afternoon
When what we feel is we remember feeling
Not long ago it was the time before

Someone sweet

Fluid, in the earth, a secret, a spill

(for H.G.)

Nocturne

"... in any way—"

—Brenda Hillman

"... prone ...."

—Marianne Moore

It was to become part of what they had
Lived without being lived through—a shared body
We had learned and were still learning about
A self-seeding not scheduled by moons

You can't say thinking of it caused the problem
Before they cooed over and over it
Or at parties sometimes people would dance
All of that once as an excuse stretched thin

One didn't try to build oneself a house
Or the grand avenue between two places
The not-quite empty lot half-wild with flowers
Somewhere they weren't really sure we wanted

Still so much to go (on) like the time when
Heralding the trumpets with someone's darkness

The sound of trumpets Harold in the darkness

"... hoard wonder and shyness ...."
                    —Brenda Hillman
"... do not matter."
                    —T. S. Eliot
"... don't understand ...."
                    —Dean Young
"... be nothing in the world ...."
                    —Richard Wilbur

Imaginations of the Ch'an Experience

"I imagine you bending ...."
                    —Brenda Hillman

Without looking the day fits into air
As we who love to be astonished note
We can let ourselves be led by a thing
To believe the very idea of vastness

No not losing the white fullness of shirts
What you carry part way to here or more
Nevermind the new red-faced and slow puffing
Morning of our inspiration in argument

To feel what we had we should always want
The ripples and clouds of the lake in turn
If the *if* were realized or a truth
As some suppose it itself a one thing
: The hills made green with winter rain and houses—
What he's going to say and what she said

"... fear ...."

—Brenda Hillman

"... fear ...."

—D. H. Lawrence

A Train Comes

Regardless of our care for openness
Some long and short of what is desire
The very idea cut at made of difference
That and there and now and here and then this

A door was where there once we were beyond
Between intervals of expected silence
In itself searching not as it seems now
The thought that time occurred that I could please

What rose was thought and what followed was not
Some crow stuck in the violet and rose and moving
Shipwrecked the moon Narcissus on a lake
Shrinking and the sound wavering hard right

Call each of the days happy under pressure
Or admit to his surprise when it comes

A small gouache

Maybe four by three

"... indistinguishable ...."
—Brenda Hillman

House, Ghost, Image, Color
Where

The command was to look—not the best thing
If you need to attach names to what comes
Out of the inner persistence to yield
A vision of something almost avoided

One rose expecting nothing much from nature
Because of the things she wanted there was
Resigned to acting in ways that you could
I escaped by means of (used) memories

Why it seems now often a call to arms
That was swallowed like a sneeze or a burp
You'd say you lived at the movies pretending
Shrubbery needed water and attention

While sky was big enough you held to it
It was the job pretty much we are starting

Give or Take

"... something else ...."

—Wallace Stevens

"Why ...."

—T. S. Eliot

Tender Burglar Stranger

"... cypress. ..."

—Marianne Moore

That silence of birds in daytime was telling
Yellow and green the second kinds of noise
Glee manifest as needles on the pine
There was also the sense that you belonged

At once your regret doesn't move you
Bread in his hands, in his beautiful hands
It is going to get hot but it rains
Black shoes stinky with frustrated design

He can't pretend you don't know how you feel
The ruined harvest taste of young Sauternes
Between your arms the body wanted too
Pain one can imagine without a hurt

Trying is a large thing inside us now
We cannot give it away ... we are trying

Baby Tears

For the first time it is impossible
Like the words *Yes* or *No* which you don't say
Or the maple turning from red to green
Nature makes and projected such indifference

On your way to water she holds herself
The cat provides a kind of displaced comfort
What you feel is more like soft tufts of grass
The deer have grazed and studded with their pellets

How is failed desire to go otherwise
We are rolling effortlessly uphill
With the consolation that pain becomes
A bunch of dropped coins once wished after him
Restlessness can be swallowed with the sound
Someone heard tell of it nears deepening

"You could pretend . . ."

> —Brenda Hillman

"The sky would not have held . . ."

> —P. J. Kavanaugh

(for Ellen Bryant Voigt)
Which Is the Dream

> ". . . there were so many . . . ."
>
> —Brenda Hillman

Back out of all this now too much for us

Let us go outside and into a distance
Making for perhaps its field behind trees

For now letting noise be noise in the road
In a barn when the cattle low their voices

Gray greening this blue to an almost green
Memory and the thing that stays a thought
In the heart of course only one and then

Meet the nice milkman with long curly lashes
Now wait for the sound of his cart and horse
Before he reached you he was singing
Out of darkness failing that once again

Both song and story full of hurrying
Farewell to the idea you don't know why

"... smoothing ... gloves. ..."
—Brenda Hillman

"I say sometimes. ..."
—Michael Ryan

"Glib Pirouette out of Messiness"
—Caroline Crumpacker

"Hoping ...."   "Weakness. ..."
—Thomas Hardy   —Carl Phillips

How do we long to think in terms of wholes
See that words don't fall to the ground together
Start across the uneven field of grass
One of us says meaning the other should
Perhaps one interest is something like safety
Hold my hand so I can look at the stars
What is at the other end of a feeling
Science between two poles a current grammar

Hold my hand I want to look at the stars
All this is too large to be seen at once
The old life and now have their own effects
Shift to grade school sixth grade being a girl
Will you go with what you have or invent
Trust in the future in your loneliness

"I love you. . . ."
                —Traditional
". . . do you love me?"
                        —Gertrude Stein
". . . I love you!"
                —Arthur Rimbaud

Late and Early Sensation

". . . progress. . . ."

                                —Dennis Cooper

Whatever he thought or used as a ladder
Beginning when as a small thing like that
The day paper slid around severed ends
One of us can start walking up the hill

Wounded or wet some bandage against it
Your muddle of pleasure wanted unsaid
We are expecting the trees to come down
A voice in Russian it is not to be

So much like that we wonder long ago
The ocher dawns and the blue summer evenings
Here again almost in the shape of you
Stutter by repeating the exhalation
Places we have liked driven past or stretching
An incomplete incapacity open

"O. . . ."
　　　　—Walt Whitman

slips

". . . one here only, the other here. . . ."
　　　　　　　—Joshua Clover

a photograph of light

Faith—The Thing with Faith
　　　　　the tenor and his vehicle

　　　　　　　　　　　　　　　". . . O . . . ."
　　　　　　　　　　　　　　　　　—Kabir

In the cracked and thickened tones of song
Hungering for what's been seen in our hands
The facts are all that matter in the world
As we more or less try to tell ourselves

The middles are lost to imagining
When you're going to watch whatever happens
To lead us through the echoes of frustration
Someone who will shout festival and June

We go on to the trails into the woods
Without believing a face will appear
Smiling in secret sometimes at ourselves
In the black-and-white coat of tweed and air

We saw them blue she said making us weep
Because of that for which some might praise us

"... just that ...."
—Robert Frost

Confusing left and right when

"... please ...."
—Walt Whitman

(Hope) and Parade

"... closer ...."
—Marianne Moore

It comes and goes in a pattern with things
By G-d in Bridgepoint no one taught the how
Was he expecting what to say yes to
We have been beasts and eaten grass ourselves

Still after no one in stretches of nothing
Why else sometimes doesn't apply you ask
Ours are blazoned on the trees in the forest
Where we might meet where we might meet again

Hot of course and of course coarse undoing
The nice guise of things falling away as
This kind our hats pushed too far sort of youth
Maybe Paris or Boston but unlikely

The wool mittens of someone else's hands
Obedient to ideas of a summer

"... my leg ...."
                        —Colette

                    "... not to mention my leg ...."
                                    —Colette

Warning

            "... lay down ...."
                —Brenda Hillman

Before or after but Not in between
            "... it was not sorrow ...."

                            —Brenda Hillman
                ("... for ... the world ...."
                            —Brenda Hillman)

But now that that's gone all tied up in light
We might as well say hello to the West
Going on to afternoons and long mornings
Where you can have a spread of good smoked fish

Now that that's gone gotten tied up in light
We can turn our attention to the West
The endless afternoon child of long mourning
And what he wants at your heart inside too

Ticky tock ticky tock disarming hello
Is every place strange or is it the company
The rest is outside you like it's earth
A thing in need of darkness for protection

We can stop and go or wait for introductions

To the light which turns to us at an angle

". . . roses."
　　　　—Colette

　　　　　　　". . . how were you to know . . . ."
　　　　　　　　　　　—Joanne Kyger

". . . orange blossoms . . . ."
　　　　—Gertrude Stein

The Maiden Several Hours Later
　　　　"Day . . . ."
　　　　　　—Jean Cocteau

To the light which turns to us at an angle
We say whatever it is that we say
Do you think someone is counting for us
How long you gonna make him wait my dear

It was all people as if having parties
If we thought we would go through it again
Perhaps it would not stay but change a little
When you said who(m) you liked with index fingers

Shaped so our hands could fit what is perfect

The astonished feeling might not subside

We think of you once up for Monday morning
In another way when with friends at night
While each one holds a big dark cup of coffee
That bird waking up to your neighbor's music

What is monologic

"... a group of children ...."
                              —Michel Leiris

choux, d'accord?

Light . . . Who Sees It
                              —Mei-mei Berssenbrugge

                    "If there are flowers ...."
                              —Brenda Hillman

left side high

You took on the plain from him in its place
Not where we could stand starts to spin and topples
She could have well before you were prepared
Only he has gone to say how it was

Under the pressure the glimpse and still counting
That one knows because once is multiple
Even in the beginning as they hope
When there was no to be telling apart

There was a need and what did you do then
Starved by some littleness to the forgotten
Banner wedges wave a lot and like this
Rain and snow figured in the course of it
As a problem could fade in our new math
Ruins part of possibility's history

"... still ...."
                —Thom Gunn

White Curtains

                              "... lay down my want ...."
                                        —Mark Wunderlich

The Hotel Room
                        " ... it would not astonish ...
              ... it would not amaze ...."
                                        —Walt Whitman

        The sun because it's grander than its light
        Stairs as part of what is hidden in seeing
        When where once again in time as if yes
        We exhale over and over the terrace

        The good arc toward a familiar gauze
        The good arc to or from the afternoon
        Washing your green walls to be free of it
        Our dark shoes tied to falling by our feet

        What he brings to air now after that habit
        A shutter opening the face of France
        They or the gardener's gate unhinged and locked
        But not with as this it our hope for it

        Break for something else quilting the ground
        You know perchance it ends in happily

"... was...."
—E. E. Cummings
"... the statue put there to persuade me ...."
—Jorie Graham

"... sit at the feet ...."
—Ron Padgett
"I like submission ...."
—Jorie Graham

A Big Long Gabled Corridor
—William Faulkner
a perfume from Ensenada

They cannot seem to bear and then escapes
Someone's always about to blame the weather
What's wrong means a sense of unpleasantness
That she loves him through our eyes can be felt

That she loves him can be seen with a look

Seeing that she loves him is a surprise

Flattened what had been was before us now

Still as if we were living at Nag's Head

You know what's wrong might be the cause of things
The endless rain without the English comforts
The important sun the laggardly shade

You know what's wrong might be the cause of things
Which will not rise . . . which will not rise again
Because it's not only our experience

"The wish . . . ."

—James Longenbach

overheard in argument

"My friend . . . ."

—Robert Bly

Yes between That Thank You
purchase your good tent

Why aren't we sold fast on the speculation
What the flower seeds and becomes the plant
That will never pass into nothingness
Two steps of concrete appear in the offing

While the fire circles around what's big here
Some ants carry themselves thousands of miles
One of us could melt at the touch of ice
Your crusade to live through late adolescence

Near the north end of a village your brother
In trade for iron railings someone's left

There were stories that we had in persistence
An out-of-date voice on the telegraph

Hello Mrs. Palumbo good night then
The edge isn't far we could be there now

". . . in stillness, even . . . ."

—James Schuyler

". . . where . . . ."

—Faiz Ahmed Faiz
(tr. Agha Shahid Ali)

Revolving toward What Is Not a Thing

"Your feet bleed . . . ."

—Faiz Ahmed Faiz
(tr. Agha Shahid Ali)

Often we park in what was once the grass
Finding it well within our opportunity
To summer alongside a softer end
Small white cards and the darkened rose of armloads

There that then may share the space of themselves
Without meaning to or remembering
One sight of before or leaving will flash
Without the wish to return our affection

The broom sweeps sometimes from a view your head
Like nights where many compared to these days
All quiet with misuse this mulch and brush
That good sense might have yielded in its turn
One red foggy car making up the road
But for our happiness and its pursuit

"... you were sitting ...."

—Peter Gizzi

"Look at the tree."

—Peter Gizzi

"I made her ...."

—Colette

Flowers on Your Path

With rain in the bank and a good prognosis
Stuck in a mouth with teeth serving as teeth
You're not often able to hasten things
Gazing at a night sky to say the name

Kingdom order phylum genus species
Out of time and against type as it happens
You're carrying a Chinese *Pi* again
There there now in your pocket in your hand

Feeding the fossil oil a gift to others
As some of those needs are held to be different
The things on the hills are probably stones
Children baring arms and their tender heads
Fish flying over us puffed up with air
However they may change from definition

"... people upstairs ...."
—Ray Suarez

"... in favor of more ...."
—Tony Hoagland

"Curiosity, Tenderness, Kindness, Ecstasy"
—Vladimir Nabokov

"Start ... now ...."
—Brenda Hillman

"... what?"
—Eugenio Montale

Yes it is hard to speak of what it was
Look how he tries to link the dots and arrows
Calling out those names we can imitate
When trees come quite easily into being

Suddenly the edge doesn't seem away
A beginning for this much of their lives
Manual diagrams might aid the drowning
Who will stand up in favor of that then

Not said the littlest one not again
Not in a chorus because of the star
Twinkling in your eyes like milk in his coffee
A note that rivals sweet dreams of wallpaper
So in our ways we have been true to someone

Happy as the darkness surrounding it

Mulberry Street

Timing
everything as
if it were cake

"Oh my love . . . ."

—Fanny Howe

". . . chairs enough . . . ."

—John Ashbery

"And then . . . and then . . . ."

—Joshua Clover

L'Histoire: Sad Chair: A History

The green's brightness (of all things) that would change
Wherein the world curls on a park and rests
That life before in months would stretch to nothing
Ivy circles beneath the blue the cedar

It began to be this more than the other
Full of fallen tree fruit and plied with nuts
Bedazzled by bits of coming attractions
The dazzle some coming attractions color

That once seems both noble and embarrassing
Someone measured the wall around the city
Each flower glimpsed in darkness its two names
A sign that seemed to bring things to their feet
As the summer was beginning or ending
What would soon become the heart of the matter

Surely

"Civilization began . . . ."
—Gertrude Stein

"Shut, shut the door, good John . . . ."
—Alexander Pope

Who Goes There?

egg and dart

Surety

Is not that place at all you say to him
Quelling all those pigs that storm on towers
Saddening looseness through magical forests
The world runs so clear of what had been once

Just enough gold and bitter greens or apples
A special friendship the shiniest ring
Who was it said *the lone and level sands*
As if it were possible to feel better

Beyond the briars there be dragons here

Something else threaded that old understanding

The figured ones have their greatness too inside

In all of what is left you feel a presence

Someone tells you what to do and you hear

All that is left to you is this a presence

Was it not a sin   "Kant thought . . . ."
                                        —Alan Stone

The Yellow Wood

"Time can look like this."
                        —Mei-mei Berssenbrugge

Lost and knowing what's carried by regret
By now so familiar time and again
Wave to this which was once a sea to us
Delight and beauty flowing out of it

Those hands motioning the air like a bird
To mark perhaps one bright sail in the distance
The blue something lifted above the garden
An invitation out the old return

We could have stumbled upon long ago
Some word from then starting what we once wanted
Taking it away from you to delay
A matter of hope for eternity
The pillow of someone once wept upon
That loss you know might become anyone

"Charlie Parker . . . ."
—Patricia Spears Jones

"Charlie Parker died . . . ."
—Patricia Spears Jones

". . . the bench is by the pond . . . ."
—Fanny Howe

Biceps of Longing

". . . from which all . . . ."
—St. Augustine

". . . for a crumb of bread."
—Toi Derricotte

As you find yourself turning now to see
There's a cloud in the pond again today
Saying that the leaves outnumber the trees
Is one more way of meaning what you want

Here and not there sometimes once then not then
As they go about this day after day
For simple reasons we are given bodies
Consider the landscape's Italian cows

Unable even to intend to yield

That fold around each encounter with nature

An essential half of this looking glass
What we can respond to and cannot fathom
Like everything from beginning to end
We would have it as it is otherwise

44

". . . odd . . . ."
— Emily Dickinson

". . . a man . . . ."
— Ralph Waldo Emerson

As If That Alone

". . . the thing intended . . . ."
— Lyn Hejinian

Seed (and) Flower

It is not now as in old days he said
Calling out to the Boy the Bright the One
It is not now what they teach and repeat
As he is to us what he is to us

We do not say leave what he is to us
What he is to us the clock has not stopped
We do not say leave so we can see now
What he is to us he is to us what

Weak in judgment still still beneath the sun
It is not now now we know that at least
We do not say so so let it be now
He is still to us what he is to us

What is he to us when he turns to us

Is a face pitiless and long delayed

"It looks like the surface . . . ."

—Mei-mei Berssenbrugge

". . . falling away from the world . . . ."

—Joshua Clover

Hesitation Step:

". . . the terror and the hungering . . . ."

—June Jordan

". . . this pair of rings . . . ."

—Marina Tsvetaeva
(tr. Catherine Ciepiela)

". . . only an hour away . . . ."

—Henry James

Of course now such seems of looseness of *un-*
We might have left to discover the world
Tethering: the heavy blackish shoes worn
When it's raining we want to reach the ground

To satisfy a need someone could imagine
Earlier having had the happy life
Like that man in the store discounting feelings
You bring yourself toward the smiles of cashiers

Once as we've begun to speak of before
We had no idea a cloud could stop
Being battened on the treetops so quickly
It reduced the distance that you can see
Between the different places on a map
Not for our one time but still under it

"... so many times ...."
                    —Johann Wolfgang von Goethe

"It makes a great difference ...."
                              —Henry James

                    what do you call it?

It Has a Back
                    —Stuart Flack
suspect from birth
                                        "... my head ...."
                                              —A. R. Ammons
              "... smiling ...."
                         —giovanni singleton

Most of all is brought back a certitude
That much depends on our own desolation
Yellow light so brittle and infinite
The flowers turn their faces up to the sky

Before it broke it was pretty as daisies
The cautionary phalanx of the police
Struck by what like us struck us all the same
Moved as we were in so many directions

For the animals we've coaxed out of hiding
It is not enough to have ridden bikes
Unless the others might borrow the carriages
This place where we are going they will share

On a good day as when it's happening
The air in fact can be carried away

"River smell . . . ."
        —Forrest Gander

". . . below us . . . above us . . .out of sight . . . ."
        —Ralph Waldo Emerson

Salvator Mundi

". . . always . . . ."   ". . . deer . . . ."
   —Michael Ondaatje   —Federico Garcia Lorca
                            (tr. Edwin Honig)

                       ". . . streets . . . ."
                           —Jean Cocteau

". . . all sorts of things . . . ."   "River smell . . . ."
     —Henry James   —Forrest Gander

        ". . . which made it beautiful."
            —Brenda Hillman

Off in again among lichens and animals
Because it is more difficult to say
Three boys in the clear American starlight
And not begin with all that will go down

Some might wish to tender their calloused hands
To take you somewhere else without delay
Spin from the darkness around which they're wound
If the path ahead seems to turn forever

The landscape does not change unlike the trees
You love we know because of that strange stillness
With no back to any of this it's clear
They had unblocked the source once and the longing
Fostered pattern made a form for the chaos
We were not required to give in so much

"It is warm . . . ."

—William Everson

". . . a certain number stick."

—Henry James

Butter Sultana Biscuits

". . . the little things . . . ."

—Robert Frost

". . . blue as the sky . . . ."

—Michael Gizzi

A glow that comes as if but from behind
That had no blood in it it was so holy
Strengthened unwillingness and disarray
In front of and against whatever happens

Like the standard fantasy you would choose
To be or not perhaps to be the ocean
Some clue because that lateness is obscured
A rain you settle into helps sustain

Those things he could not find while we were able
Spectacles all along the levee road
So what would come around was perfect fortune
A need for distance greater than this room
A way you know we could be certain of
Depending on again for years ahead

"There is a space . . . ."
>—Mei-mei Berssenbrugge

"You find a space . . . ."
>—Mei-mei Berssenbrugge

"The object is the space . . . ."
>—Peter Gizzi

". . . go on . . . ."
>—D. A. Powell

Fantasie C–dur

". . . the sound . . . ."
>—Ann Lauterbach

The bigness scented the trees as expected
The earth felt masculine during the burning
The beginning of evening could be pretty
This pretty evening we did not expect

When we remembered we'd remind ourselves
A sequence of small things was going on
Quite far away in a neighboring county
We were just tall enough to see the effects

Quite far away in the neighboring county
In some sequence small things were going on
When we remembered to remind ourselves
We had no need to speculate on causes

The bigness was masculine and expected
Some trees we could see were pulling us closer

That Rose before Me

Here if the two of us had ever been
There would come a rider on a pale horse
Who would look at you with a different face
A curious illusion O well beloved

If there could be a story to wash off
The other gold we know as dirt and grime
What within us the light converts to red
Were it all possible we could begin

The kind words you said to the other people
A past gesture or fragrance softly fall
The course is timed with books of tiny flowers
In place with once what you had been given
—And the water looking over your shoulder
Where it might have been better all the same

"It is not important."

—Eleanor Clark

"But it was October . . . ."

—Jon Anderson

What Remains Comfort

"... simply) so conspicuously . . . ."

—John Fowles

"... we become motionless . . . ."

—Gaston Bachelard

A fragment of what they believe exists
In your thinking even so of our madness
As traps of light that move toward each surface
Stopped us from saying somehow more and more

Could they have had it once it was allowed
Or don't things work like that within as rhythms
In the way like some other way of wanting
As ought might enter into your own garden

If it weren't possible to lack elsewhere
Losing the long days to their well-fed shadows
No one that we know of would try or bother
The world you see its picture is a portrait
Thanks perhaps to that nice man on a trip
Giving us besides now what we have here

"... the present of a lie ...."
                                      —Colette

            "Racine found it possible ...."
                                      —W. Somerset Maugham

After the work the painter felt so sad

Those Things which Were Not Ambiguities

                        "... hold now to your ear ...."
                                      —Jorie Graham
                "... the earth ...."
                                      —John Koethe
"... everything moves ...."
                —Wallace Stevens

It seemed to be the defining event
All of that in a dream they had or once
One smooth-coated and one rough-coated bull
Which you understood was inaccurate

By the time they reached the point with a corner
And a bridge over a river you'd cross
Delighted by the quality of voices
Saying good-bye to that which could not be

You struck out on your own search for perfection
And soon found quelle surprise nothing so shapely
You had stopped singing for a time out loud

You had stopped slowly beginning to notice
And while that was happening you continued
Without having to decide things would last

A Feeling in the Countryside

"... jasmines would fill ...."
—Federico Garcia Lorca
(tr. Edwin Honig)

"Forgive me ...."
—Anne Sexton

Natural and Imaginary Objects

| the sunflower | square | cut | envelope | all |
| the traveler | moistened | few | segments | lining |

"... the exponent ...."
—Emily Dickinson

Even as then they are not accurate
In size or composition of a range
With such as can seem to surmount the fact
And you as has been true for many years

In part more giving there at kindliness
Withstood again a storm along the road
But this as it seems today yet again
Might believing grow only out of it

Who was to declare what you were once thinking
We cannot bring ourselves to that account
Or how in the series of so it is
Souls are seen changing the earth colors rooms

Now was to be something so unlike this

Surely somewhere although it is not known

"... gesture ...."

—Jean Cocteau

"... gestures ...."

—W. Somerset Maugham

"... gesture ...."

—E. E. Cummings

Apparatus for Distillation

In the world in which there is no one hoping
But as a strange plenitude with for trees
The stones breaking broken into small stones
What bits of them brighten make shells and glass
Like stars waves unbending the bands of light
Of sweet to flowering and fruited bareness
So that there is that in you grand in feeling
Alive a need turned to well as a thing
Or the man for whom once there were the women
Seen then in that difference swimming and home
So there the end this closing beauty brothers
All of that then in alchemical tones
Have each from the other silence a blessing
What is still in us there as that our feeling
In that world which is there is always hoping

Good-bye Abel's quiet blessing

"... goodbye is the operative word ...."

—Peter Gizzi

"... all-embracing ...."
　　　　　　—Thomas Hardy

　　　　　　　　"... open again ...."
　　　　　　　　　　　—John Ashbery

The Rescue Party
　　　　"... the sun in January ...."
　　　　　　　　—Greg Miller

"... you will see them ...."　　　　　　　"... they cry easily ...."
　　　—W. Somerset Maugham

　　　　　　　　　　　　　　goes on

It has come so slowly to be with us
A testament or jars of milk and honey
Like now with again some feeling ourselves
So that everything can wash over you

Whoever they are on the road in passing
Jonquils and narcissi almost enough
The colors as we called them have not lessened
Because of this having craving to sense

Not in manner unlike you hesitant
How that thing holds and when cannot be named
So deer august possibility beckons
Still not yet trying to forget your body
The sound of things we cannot hear stop
Though there are wilds of leading one astray

Cape Cod

border of earth

"... kettle ...."   "... the right ...."
—W. Somerset Maugham   —Jean Cocteau

patterns   room

"... feeling ...."
—Elizabeth Barrett Browning

"... in the dark ...."
—Joan Acocella

whatever the time of day or night

"... patterns of feeling ...."
—Eleanor Clark

Pail of Water

"... praise their yellow breasts ...."
—Greg Miller

It's arranged and things are about to brighten
The waterslide sounds as it is supposed
Our eyes grow still more familiar with longing
Here in the world and not that long ago

Say that we are walking and holding hands
Just as the cypress makes a day for us
Or tones of weeping lead some wall away
For what is there perhaps now fades to red

An honor or nail might each moment deepen
The light passing over things it has known
We may soon not even ourselves remember
To feel our wandering here as the end

It might stay for a while if you asked it to
It might stay for a long while if it's possible

Look up!

—Paul Eluard

"... broken ...."

—Eleanor Clark

Undisturbing Distance

"They have done things ...."

—Mark Wunderlich

We acted happily and found the party
Time was out stretching itself by the lake
A feeling we had would not settle down
It had come so slowly to be with us

Once we almost dropped something we'd been doing
Before began to look the other way
Everyone was polite or did not notice
When we thought it was time to say good-bye

It mattered to us greatly that we see
Like now much else we were hearing about
One side of the thing we would soon discover
As though until then it was not all ours

It was something but it was still not light
It could be given and taken away

"... the ...."
—Sophie Cabot Black

it pours
"... in ...."
—Sophie Cabot Black

Another Happy Story
never very far

The tear he had said needed to be mended
And our lips parted so the tongue could move
We were still in the room and we were happy
We were still in the dark and it was good

Although there was that so-called irritant
We passed it kindly between our dry hands
What had seemed too long now was growing short
We could taste what we had tasted before

About all this of it that went so well
Having is the boomerang for that time
Having made the fly skip across the lake
Having had and had and had it evolved
Hearing the laughter and longing you know
We might talk about it being forever

penny-colored bubblegum

"... come inside ...."
—Elizabeth Willis

Perhaps No Longer Than That All

"... unknown ...."
—John Masefield

We have been well served by that all ourselves
Always for us everywhere afternoon
You know that immense understanding yes
We can feel when we think of that then

Could it be called still your sun or the moon
That view of the world every window opened
Called into this though once as it went out
If it were not as we would as it is

A train is pulling now away from here
And someone flowering the tables trees
There may be quiet sometimes and a stir
That evening never stops from closing in

You try to remember it's not the same
You see this way of being disappeared

"... sugar to the wind ...."
—Randall Jarrell

Where do you stay?

"Night dark ...."
—Sophie Cabot Black

Wherever We Are Going Are We Almost

There
        was an injury in the course of
Things
        we were to know later were not yet
Known
        in a way that would continue the
Feeling
        we were trying to hold onto
Was
        for us all that time a way of being
What
        we had been dreaming we might become
One
        of the impossible things we always
Wanted
        like music which again it seemed
Moved
        by that before we were falling into
Quickly
        so that what was wrong was no longer
As
        likely for us as what we had once
Thought
        we would be happy and joy would carry
Over
        all the things we might have wished for
Ourselves
        the experience of this still

"It was everything . . . ."
—Wallace Stevens

". . . sweet to weep for . . . ."
—Claire Malroux
(tr. Marilyn Hacker)

John Button Has a Pretty Name

". . . is . . . ."
—Gertrude Stein

There is this place where we wanted to live
The sky a pretty color moves along
As it is sometimes we feel that again
There may not be much use in our pretending
The land could itself increase in its worth
Just as we are called far out into this
Mountainous abstractions might form and cloud
The ink-darkened trees then reshape themselves

Let your friends step back and admire the world
That hue and cry signal for all it is
Like wild geese or grasses bent in splendor
A strand of hair in the raspberry canes

It is not one of the things left behind
So as there it continues on for us

Mary's Pond

through

"... before it can begin ...."

—Henry Darger (quoted by John D'Agata)

People, the Woods

"Lie down ...."

—Forrest Gander

The worldly remains   to be left behind
Probably it is still   itself a shape
          Like the dark sky no longer hovering
It can't be that   it had so much to do

What is being made room for now   in this
No one says that you have to start   again
          It could be never now the next time
Perhaps it's found outside   a place to rest

It might be that other plans have been laid
For fulfillment or something even nicer
We aren't sure if we'd use the word ourselves
But with our knack for forgetting it's likely
It had come to us once before   we smiled
We didn't know what to say we said
                         Hello

Mary's Pond

~~~~~~~~~~~~~~~~~~~~~~~~~~~

through

Two People in the Woods

The thing is often in the way of feeling
It doesn't really matter how it started
Some moments may be marked by afternoons
Because of yes that French bouquet of flowers
Most people go outside to grow and love

We have come to admire what we could admire
Perhaps the understory bears repeating
Masses of berries in the shade you see
So the thin light does not fall any closer
So we have this still within easy reach

We may go on as if we do not know
Because of yes because of all the flowers
We were tempted to follow ever after
Whatever we find is it . . . our reward

set them out

For One Instance

Going into what we have (so long) called
A turning of like (you say) yes the back
You know the world (inside) has captured us
And that (again) nothing may now be lost

Full (because) of what you felt would not happen
We began (in time) to dream of those things
That might have been (somewhere) waiting for us
Just as perhaps (our own) ideas of this

Finding (the way) ourselves with tiny steps
We shall go on (we know) as in the past
Whatever (you think) you want close at hand

We came to (love) this strange place with our wanting
For what indeed (it seems) was never ours
Still we'll go on (as if) we cannot stop

Hotel-Title: Poem

There's that which we remember as good-bye
While some other thing led us here to this
Would we be foolish to hope for a change
Still our hope for a change that is not foolish

What was given to us seemed to be trouble
There were a few worries that came and went
There were other worries that lived with us
And while we searched for answers they did not

Could it be perhaps that we've misremembered
What did you say to the people you saw
We want to know what we want and we want
Without letting love enter into it
A new way of being constantly modeled
So the choice before us appears as open

"... bear ... knowing ...."
—Rainer Maria Rilke

"A bird sang ...."
—Theodore Roethke

Continuous: Interruption

walk with honeysuckle

Because the cities appear to you changing
We might as well begin and paint the sky
The bluff and the hill are modes of well being
And lift our eyes to whatever astounds

From here to there with that again in us
So soon it may come to be what we call
A moment of undoing someone had
Now that all this and more can be alone

You do not have to try to stop sensation
Unless you feel it has no afterlife
We are given this continuing present
Even underneath things it may be still
So much like this that is which it becomes
A sense in part can get carried along

"The road . . . ."   ". . . then becomes continuous . . . ."
        —George Oppen   —John Koethe

            ". . . in the distance . . . ."
                        —Athol Fugard

". . . closest . . . ."   ". . . the sea . . . ."
        —Yoko Ono   —Athol Fugard

A Temporary Spot

                        ". . . travelled . . . ."
                              —E. E. Cummings

When you go out of doors there is the spring
Giving up your attachment to the absence
How pretty things are when you stop you notice
We went about the world as if it were
Forgetting that it might have had a purpose
Again in time you might come to think that
One could begin by finishing what's left
It's been quite a while since whatever happened
Whatever it was we knew it could go
Even if it had never been announced
You could not be bothered to try to change
As before you thought when it would not end
It may not be at all as if each time
Courting still only what appears to be

"You go to a place . . . ."
—Ann Lauterbach

"And then some more time passes . . . ."
—Claudia Rankine

In Berlin: Secret Agent Man

". . . in Berlin . . . ."
—Campbell McGrath

Still

Now

Unerring as rain that is slowly falling
You waited outside the impossible
For a long time you did not want to be
Holding the shell of some emptiness
The emptiness you guarded . . . in your mind
It might have gone off in a quiet way
Surprising you when it did not appear
Happy as you were with its needing you

Rolled inside that tight volumetric longing
News had come from a pretty distant heaven
You could see all the things you had been missing
You left so you could be right in the middle
One again with so many other things
That became really difficult to bear

"... Harry learned ...."
                                    —Robin Blaser

"He hadn't seen the tree ...."
                                    —Susan Stewart

more than once

We Said to Someone

                                                        blue
                                                    cashmere

                                                     church

                    "... another day ...."
                                    —Forrest Hamer

            It had because to be like what went on
            So ensconced were we in the eastern hills
            The trees were one minute that did not bother
            And then you were still somehow that transformed

            Already it was as they saw beginning
            Through to something that was not for you but
            Before when we had chosen now recalled
            In its way of course all of our depending

            Adding yes onto what some might call this
            Again because you know it is not all
            Fraught with what could be possible in feeling
            Quite far really away from us in fact

            When it seemed impossible you were perfect
            To let it remain as it was ... so perfect

is it not

Morning Coat

"... sweet ...."
        —William Carlos Williams

painted blue

You feel it has stayed so now for these months
Among all those in the same room with singing
Not the way it is what you had been wanting
Although it was as you saw nothing else

How it was you know it began to be
The feeling stopped by again had not changed
One route he showed them led you far from there
So there was that quite continually

You did not wish for more than time to turn
Everlasting still yet not as it seemed
To put facts in place with certain particulars
Many of the children could purse their lips

To think with your hands you'd clear a great forest
More surprisingly though you made it home

wide   wide

"... Emma ...."   "... Paul ...."
             —Charles Darwin   —Norman Mailer

wide wide

Drift
Land

I think it never evaporates

Indeed there were planes to your mild surprise
Before you had known what it was you wanted
That filled rooms with a kind of happiness
Then there were many possibilities

So it could be you thought the way it was
Thinking of the first time we turned away
You went in awed in the hope it would help
Whatever it was that was about to happen

We thought we had something and let it go

The world had shown you how it could be done

That might have been seen as breaking the surface

Still we leaned quite far forward to see if

It was true over time that you'd feel nothing

Ever after could be this beautiful

About the Author

A featured poet-performer in New York's Panasonic Village Jazz Fest and a decorated veteran of the slam-poetry scene, poet and translator G. E. PATTERSON is the author previously of *Tug* (Graywolf Press), winner of the Minnesota Book Award. He lives and teaches in the Minneapolis–St. Paul area and holds degrees from Princeton and Stanford universities.

Ahsahta Press

SAWTOOTH POETRY PRIZE SERIES

2002: Aaron McCollough, *Welkin* (Brenda Hillman, judge)

2003: Graham Foust, *Leave the Room to Itself* (Joe Wenderoth, judge)

2004: Noah Eli Gordon, *The Area of Sound Called the Subtone* (Claudia Rankine, judge)

2005: Karla Kelsey, *Knowledge, Forms, The Aviary* (Carolyn Forché, judge)

2006: Paige Ackerson-Kiely, *In No One's Land* (D. A. Powell, judge)

2007: Rusty Morrison, *the true keeps calm biding its story* (Peter Gizzi, judge)

NEW SERIES

1. Lance Phillips, *Corpus Socius*
2. Heather Sellers, *Drinking Girls and Their Dresses*
3. Lisa Fishman, *Dear, Read*
4. Peggy Hamilton, *Forbidden City*
5. Dan Beachy-Quick, *Spell*
6. Liz Waldner, *Saving the Appearances*
7. Charles O. Hartman, *Island*
8. Lance Phillips, *Cur aliquid vidi*
9. Sandra Miller, *oriflamme.*
10. Brigitte Byrd, *Fence Above the Sea*
11. Ethan Paquin, *The Violence*
12. Ed Allen, *67 Mixed Messages*
13. Brian Henry, *Quarantine*
14. Kate Greenstreet, *case sensitive*
15. Aaron McCollough, *Little Ease*
16. Susan Tichy, *Bone Pagoda*
17. Susan Briante, *Pioneers in the Study of Motion*
18. Lisa Fishman, *The Happiness Experiment*
19. Heidi Lynn Staples, *Dog Girl*
20. David Mutschlecner, *Sign*
21. Kristi Maxwell, *Realm Sixty-Four*
22. G. E. Patterson, *To and From*
23. Chris Vitiello, *Irresponsibility*

Ahsahta Press

Modern and Contemporary Poetry of the American West

Sandra Alcosser, *A Fish to Feed All Hunger*

David Axelrod, *Jerusalem of Grass*

David Baker, *Laws of the Land*

Dick Barnes, *Few and Far Between*

Conger Beasley, Jr., *Over DeSoto's Bones*

Linda Bierds, *Flights of the Harvest-Mare*

Richard Blessing, *Winter Constellations*

Boyer, Burmaster, and Trusky, eds., *The Ahsahta Anthology*

Peggy Pond Church, *New and Selected Poems*

Katharine Coles, *The One Right Touch*

Wyn Cooper, *The Country of Here Below*

Craig Cotter, *Chopstix Numbers*

Judson Crews, *The Clock of Moss*

H. L. Davis, *Selected Poems*

Susan Strayer Deal, *The Dark is a Door*

Susan Strayer Deal, *No Moving Parts*

Linda Dyer, *Fictional Teeth*

Gretel Ehrlich, *To Touch the Water*

Gary Esarey, *How Crows Talk and Willows Walk*

Julie Fay, *Portraits of Women*

Thomas Hornsby Ferril, *Anvil of Roses*

Thomas Hornsby Ferril, *Westering*

Hildegarde Flanner, *The Hearkening Eye*

Charley John Greasybear, *Songs*

Corrinne Hales, *Underground*

Hazel Hall, *Selected Poems*

Nan Hannon, *Sky River*

Gwendolen Haste, *Selected Poems*

Kevin Hearle, *Each Thing We Know Is Changed Because We Know It And Other Poems*

Sonya Hess, *Kingdom of Lost Waters*

Cynthia Hogue, *The Woman in Red*

Robert Krieger, *Headlands, Rising*

Elio Emiliano Ligi, *Disturbances*

Haniel Long, *My Seasons*

Ken McCullough, *Sycamore•Oriole*

Norman MacLeod, *Selected Poems*

Barbara Meyn, *The Abalone Heart*

David Mutschlecner, *Esse*

Dixie Partridge, *Deer in the Haystacks*

Gerrye Payne, *The Year-God*

George Perreault, *Curved Like an Eye*

Howard W. Robertson, *to the fierce guard in the Assyrian Saloon*

Leo Romero, *Agua Negra*

Leo Romero, *Going Home Away Indian*

Miriam Sagan, *The Widow's Coat*

Philip St. Clair, *At the Tent of Heaven*

Philip St. Clair, *Little-Dog-of-Iron*

Donald Schenker, *Up Here*

Gary Short, *Theory of Twilight*

D. J. Smith, *Prayers for the Dead Ventriloquist*

Richard Speakes, *Hannah's Travel*

Genevieve Taggard, *To the Natural World*

Tom Trusky, ed., *Women Poets of the West*

Marnie Walsh, *A Taste of the Knife*

Bill Witherup, *Men at Work*

Carolyne Wright, *Stealing the Children*

This book is set in Apollo MT type with FF Scala Sans titles
by Ahsahta Press at Boise State University
and manufactured according to the Green Press Initiative
by Thomson-Shore, Inc.
Cover design by Quemadura.
Book design by Janet Holmes.

AHSAHTA PRESS
2008

JANET HOLMES, DIRECTOR
STEFFEN BROWN
NAOMI TARLE
J R WALSH
DENNIS BARTON, INTERN
DALE SPANGLER, INTERN